Cheyenne Martin
9465 Wilshire Blvd., Suite 300
Beverly Hills, CA 90212
www.cheyennemartin.com

Emerald City Entertainment
www.emeraldcity.film

Cheyenne Martin Foundation
www.cheyennemartinfoundation.org

AuthorHouse™
1663 Liberty Drive
Bloomington, IN 47403
www.authorhouse.com
Phone: 1 (800) 839-8640

Cover & Interior Design:
Sean Michael Beyer

Proofreaders:
Nick Pasqual and Frederick Mintchell

Cover Photos:
Tyrone Richardson

Makeup Artist:
Leyvi K. Villagran

Stylist:
Tessa James

ISBN: 978-1-7283-0967-5 (sc)
ISBN: 978-1-7283-0968-2 (e)

Library of Congress Control Number: 2019906368

Print information available on the last page.

Published by AuthorHouse 03/03/2020

authorHOUSE

I would like to lovingly dedicate this book, first to my maternal grandmother Mary Martin,

who helped me grow up to be the strong woman I have become.

She always taught me to defeat what's trying to defeat you.

Heartfelt dedications as well to my inspiring paternal grandmother Iola Bowie,

and my mother Wanda Bowie and my father Donnie Bowie, thank you for giving me life.

In Loving Memory of Marqese J. Tann

CHEYENNE MARTIN

Reclaiming My Strength

How a mystery illness, tragic loss and, devastating news, became a positive, life-changing experience.

Contents

My name is Cheyenne Martin.

ONE

Something's Very Wrong

I'VE WORKED in some form of the entertainment business ever since I moved from Pittsburgh to Los Angeles in 1986. From acting, supporting my son Dre's acting career, as an agent's assistant, a personal manager, executive producer and eventually a producer with my own production company, Emerald City Entertainment, Inc., I've always been a strong, tenacious person with the drive and determination to succeed.

I thought nothing could stop me until the beginning of March of 2015 when I'd developed a slight limp as I was walking. I had no idea what caused it, but I figured it would eventually subside.

I was wrong.

As the month wore on, I started to notice my legs were aching at night when I was in bed. They'd be curving inward and when I tried to straighten them, it was uncomfortable and sore. One morning I awoke to my right knee cap swollen to the size of a grapefruit. It was scary; I didn't know what was going on. As it progressed, walking became increasingly strenuous and laborious. Mornings were the hardest. I'd wake up to go to the bathroom and it was like I was handicapped. I would pray that it would be gone the next day. But it was the same thing each morning and progressively got worse. I'd have to balance myself on chairs, against a wall, whatever I could hold onto to lessen the pressure on my legs so I could move just a few feet to the bathroom. I honestly thought that I was going to be crippled. I thought I was going to be deformed and look hideous. It scared me to death.

At the time, I was working on this serial killer film and doing research, as well as reading an intense book for the project. I was in a mentally dark place as it was, and with my health apparently beginning to decline, it became a very wearisome time. I was frustrated. I felt ashamed. I didn't know what to do and I didn't want anyone to know anything was wrong. I just kept moving along with life like everything was okay.

My boyfriend Marqese and I were living together and I'd always get up before him or sometimes slept in the guest bedroom so he wouldn't know there was an issue. Finally, one day I had to ask him if he noticed if anything looked wrong and he said, "No. Baby, you're the healthiest person I know." Indeed. I was always very active. Horseback riding, hiking, playing nine or eighteen holes of golf, skeet shooting, jet skiing, boxing. You name it, I did it. Although he did notice my right knee was swollen, he brushed it off. He told me I was "tripping" and it was nothing to worry about. That was not what I wanted to hear. I needed him to see that there was an issue that should be addressed immediately.

Instead he told me to quit babying my knee, get out and walk. Essentially, he suggested I "man up," if you will, sometimes even yelling at me about it. I was so irritated and frustrated with him.

We know our bodies better than anyone and we know when things don't feel or seem right. And for him not to show concern, was not only devastating, it was emotionally debilitating.

The stress at the time began to spiral out of control. I'd just closed my management company and was focusing on producing and getting a film funded, along with various other projects at different stages of development. Combined with a toxic personal relationship and an unknown health issue, this time was taxing beyond anything I'd ever experienced. Marqese and I had broken up, gotten back together, broken up again, too many times. One day, I'd finally had enough and ended it. It was over. It was over for good. I still cared about him. I still loved him, but we couldn't be together. It was just too difficult and unhealthy. It hurt my heart, but I had to say goodbye.

DAY-TO-DAY TASKS BECAME CUMBERSOME. Any time I was sitting still for maybe twenty minutes or more, it would be arduous just to stand. I dreaded driving to the store. By the time I got there, I'd be stiff again and found it excruciating just to get out of the car as my feet landed on the pavement. Once I was moving, once the blood was circulating, it wasn't as bad. It was still painful, but at least I could move to some degree.

No longer being the active person I was once, was upsetting, sad and so very depressing, I felt like a prisoner in my own body. But I've always been strong. Anyone who knows me, knows I'm an alpha-female! I was determined. I wasn't going to let this stop me. Even though I didn't know what was happening to my body, I knew I was going to beat it one way or another. In hindsight, I probably should've told others what was happening, but my pride prevented that. I didn't want to appear to be weak.

I'd have lunch meetings with my entertainment business colleagues and I'd always arrive early. First step was to get situated at a table before anyone else arrived. We'd have our meeting, enjoy our lunch, chat for a bit, then after we paid the check, I'd make up an excuse to stay after so they wouldn't see how grueling it was for me to simply get up out of my seat. I guess you'd call it a work around, so no one knew anything was wrong. But it was embarrassing when I'd have to ask our server for his hand to pull me up. Image is important and I didn't want mine to appear to be anything less than perfect. One can say that's vain, and perhaps it is to some degree, but "show biz" is not for the meek and I was determined to get better, beat this whatever it was, and then no one would be the wiser.

I had no idea at the time, but this was the beginning of a new and quite different chapter of my life. I'd started doing a great deal of research based upon my symptoms. I found they matched rheumatoid arthritis, osteoporosis, lupus, even forms of cancer. I thought I had everything! I thought I was dying. I thought this was it. Which is exactly why one should not self-diagnose with Dr. Google!

First, I went to see the Chinese herbalist, Dr. Ho in Van Nuys, a suburb of Los Angeles in the San Fernando Valley. I would walk in, with my knees were pointed inward and bent. Both were swollen; one more than the other. He treated the pain in my knees with acupuncture twice a week. It would feel better for a few hours, but then the pain and stiffness would return. I was also having hour-long Swedish massage sessions, three times a week. Anything to keep the pain at bay.

My next step was to see an orthopedic doctor. He performed various tests and told me the cartilage in my knees was thinning and he prescribed Synvisc[1], which is for osteoarthritis[2]. I had to have four shots in each knee at a cost of $350 each—with no insurance! And even when I finally got insurance, they wouldn't cover it! I had no choice but to pay for the shots; I had to get better. I was happy though. If the problem was osteoarthritis, I could live with that. They were pricey, but these shots were going to make me better!

If only that were true.

Although the shots did help and I was in less pain, I later discovered it was sort of like putting a Band Aid on a gaping wound. I have no ill will towards this doctor, even to this day. He thought he was providing the proper treatment, as did I. I began to receive physical therapy and continued with the very expensive weekly knee injections.

Nonetheless, I was starting to feel better and it seemed as though things were moving in a positive direction. The pain in my knees was significantly less, but they were stiff as a board and felt like they weighed twice as much as they did. And since I'd grown accustomed to being helped up, I literally had forgotten how to stand on my own.

Then I got the call. A call no one should ever have to receive.

My ex-boyfriend Marqese had been brutally murdered.

---

[1]*Synvisc or Synvisc-One® (hylan G-F 20) is indicated for the treatment of pain in osteoarthritis (OA) of the knee in patients who have failed to respond adequately to conservative non-pharmacologic therapy and simple analgesics, e.g., acetaminophen. (Source: WebMD)*

[2]*Osteoarthritis (OA) is the most common form of arthritis, affecting millions of people worldwide. It occurs when the protective cartilage on the ends of your bones wears down over time. Although osteoarthritis can damage any joint in your body, the disorder most commonly affects joints in your hands, knees, hips and spine. (Source: WebMD)*

2015 was a year of misery, pain

and devastating heartbreak.

TWO

Love Hurts

I'VE ALWAYS BEEN VERY SPIRITUAL. I regularly pray and ask God for guidance. I've also been one to have visions, premonitions; many have even said I'm clairvoyant. Perhaps I'm just in tune with the energy of the universe.

Early in 2015, I had this vision in the middle of the day that Marqese and I were hogtied in our bedroom. There were two others in the room, but all I could see was their feet and legs, nothing else. I knew they were going to kill us. It was terrifying. I said to him, "This is it!" After a moment, I looked into his eyes and whispered, "I love you." Then just as quickly as the vision appeared, it came to end. I thought to myself, I can't be with him. Something is going to happen. Something serious. Something life-changing. Something life-ending.

Marqese was ridiculously charming. One of those wild and mysterious "bad boys" with piercing eyes that looked deep into your soul. He and I had a strong bond. We'd been together since 2011 and had some amazing times together, with an equal amount of bad ones as well. (I'd like to look back at the good times as fond memories, but that's nearly impossible to do now.) To say he was no angel, is an understatement.

He did have good qualities, but the dark side of him and those he associated with far outweighed any possible good. He was everything you've seen in "gangsta" movies, only very real. Very dangerous.

Over the years, I'd seen a holistic doctor and he thought the stress of living with Marqese and the unhealthy relationship was what brought on, I would later learn, was my mystery illness. It was already in my body, but probably would've remained dormant for many more years had my life been less stressful.

When I was with Marqese, I was continuously looking over my shoulder, checking my surroundings, constantly afraid something was going to happen at any moment. Once he arrived home for the night, I'd make sure all the doors and windows were locked in the house; I had cameras everywhere, motion sensors and two elaborate alarm systems. I was always fearful someone would follow him home or lay in wait for him and I'd be caught in the middle—an innocent victim guilty by association. I even had an emergency plan that if someone were to break into the house, I would hide in the attic until it was safe. I went so far as to take firearm lessons so I could safely protect myself.

I'd break up with him and he'd come back a short while later. Time and time again. He wouldn't take no for an answer. He was out of control and manipulative. He was so desperate to win me back. Finally, that July, I was able to break free of him. It was over and that was that. No contact. No more drama.

Or so I thought.

He owned a marijuana dispensary in Compton, which is in the heart of South Central Los Angeles, not the best part of town whatsoever.

September the 19th was the last time I saw Marqese. He said he was coming to pick up his clothes and belongings, but that was not his intention. Once he arrived, he told me he loved me and missed our Sundays. He missed us being together. Sundays had always been our day. We'd go out to dinner or I would cook or we would do something special. He kept saying he wanted to come home and start over. He wasn't the type of guy to be soft, but this night he said, "I'm coming at you as soft as I can." It was very sweet, until he went on to say that if another man came around, he'd kill him and me. "You don't play with a real nigga like me, I'll kill you." I didn't argue with him, I just listened. I don't know how, perhaps divine intervention, but I eventually got him to calm down and we talked until he had to leave for his shop. I think my body language and energy told him it was really over between us, perhaps not. But he left nonetheless.

I breathed a momentary sigh of relief, but sensed that something just wasn't right. I sat down to watch some television and then a wash of emotions came over me. My eyes went black and I had a vision of Marqese laying sideways, his head in a pool of blood. It terrified me and I called my friend Kieren, hysterical. Her first inclination was that he'd hurt me somehow. I assured her that wasn't the case, but through streaming tears, I told her about the vision I'd just had and shouted, "He's not going to make it, he's not going to make it!" I knew his life was in danger and there was nothing I could do about it.

On September 22, starting at about 2pm, Marqese began texting me: "Eyes on you, Baby"; "I love you, I miss you"; and "I'm coming home tonight." I woke up around 2:30am and he wasn't home, nor had he called or sent a text. I was somewhat relieved, but I was also worried something had happened.

This is one time I prayed to God I was wrong.

IT WAS SEPTEMBER 23RD. At 8:45pm, I got a call from my friend Amanda to turn on the news. There had been a shooting at a dispensary in Compton and two men were dead. I grabbed the remote, changed the channel and there was his car. I immediately tried calling and texting him, over and over. There was no response.

I knew it was him. I knew he was inside. I knew he was dead.

At 3am, I received confirmation Marqese and his friend had been murdered inside his dispensary, shot point blank in the head.

I was devastated. Oh the pain. I can't even describe the gut-wrenching cries that came from deep within my soul. I cried like I've never cried before. My heart was deeply wounded. The man that I loved was gone. It was the kind of pain I had never experienced in my life. I was inconsolable.

I was heartbroken.

The grieving was real. Letting go of him was even more real. So many days and nights filled with tears, wondering what could have been if we had given it one more chance to try and be happy together. I know I probably should've tried to move on with my life, but I wasn't ready.

And now, my mystery illness had become the worst it had ever been.

If it was God's will for me to be crippled;

If it was his will for me to be in a wheelchair, so be it.

But if there was a way for me to fight...

I was gonna fight!

THREE

Moving Forward

THE SATURDAY FOLLOWING MARQESE'S DEATH, I took a trip to my cousin's home in Victorville; about a 90 minute drive from Los Angeles. I needed support. I was overwhelmed. I needed to be around my family. I was having an incredibly hard time dealing with his murder.

But once I arrived, I didn't want to go inside.

I remained in my truck while on the phone with Marqese's sister, going over a few things pertaining to his funeral. Shortly after we ended the call, the toes on my right foot suddenly sprung backward, pointing up towards me. It was bizarre. It was scary. I had no clue what had caused this. After about two minutes, I pulled the hair tie from my ponytail and wrapped it around my toes. I tried to pull them back, but they wouldn't budge. I was in shock and didn't know what to do. Why was this happening?

Ten minutes passed and finally they went back to normal. I knew something was seriously wrong with me. But I knew I had to help deal with Marqese's funeral first. I'd never discussed this with anyone, it was just too uncomfortable and awkward. I later discovered this spasm can be brought on for a variety of reasons, especially extreme stress. And I was stressed!

It was time to lay Marqese to rest, and I was there to assist his family with the arrangements. I made sure everything he wore from head to toe was brand new and looked good. Many of my friends couldn't believe that I was doing this. We'd had such a tumultuous relationship and most turned their backs on me. I was really disappointed. My heart was hurting and I knew they didn't like him, but I needed them to be there for me and they weren't. However, I knew deep down that it was the right thing to do. I knew God would honor that.

Only two of my close friends were supportive. Kieren showed me unconditional love. I was afraid to sleep at home, so I stayed with her for many nights. Words weren't necessary as it was understood what I needed. She offered me her bed while she slept on the couch. I quietly sobbed for hours until eventually I fell asleep. Come morning, I'd give her a hug and head back home.

My friend Chasity was always checking on me, making sure I was doing okay. She even offered to be there for me at the funeral; but I knew I had to do that on my own.

I couldn't have made it through this difficult time without them.

Two months before he was murdered, he and I were in the kitchen having breakfast and he said, "If anything happens to me, make sure I'm buried right." It was important that I honored his wishes. There was no question that I was going to be there day and night to assist his family with making sure he was laid to rest with dignity. He was far from perfect and had many flaws, but he did love me and I loved him. I knew it was right in my heart and I felt it my responsibility to make sure he was given respect, which in turn gave me closure. It gave me the ability to move on with my life and focus on healing, both emotionally and physically.

But I was exhausted.

EVERY DAY I FELT LIKE GIVING UP. Each morning, when it was a struggle just to go to the bathroom, I felt like staying in bed; but I knew I couldn't. I knew I had to fight. And I knew I was going to be alone. I still didn't want anyone to know. That's not what I want. That's not who I am. I don't want sympathy. Sympathy is for the weak. That's why I kept it to myself. I was going to beat this. I was going to stay the course. I was going to be physically strong again.

It was shortly after Thanksgiving and my health was rapidly declining. I would lay awake at night because the pain had spread to my neck, hands, back and left elbow. It was unbearable to sleep. It was overwhelming. Mornings consisted of drawing a hot bath to soak and soothe my stiff joints just to get around during the day with a little less pain. Very little. My wrists were so weak, I'd ask my son Dre to come over to open jars, take out the trash—household duties that most of us take for granted. Simple chores we take for granted until they're nearly impossible to do.

Christmas was around the corner and I was still mourning Marqese. But I was going to celebrate my favorite holiday no matter what.

Shopping was such a daunting task. I'd head to the mall and wouldn't be able to walk more than fifteen steps before I'd have to rest. It was tedious and exhausting. My body was failing me and it appeared there was nothing I could do about it.

I had to stand in this extremely long check out line and I recognized this well-known actress. We made eye contact and she could tell I was in pain. She smiled and asked if everything was okay. I shook my head. I reluctantly said no. To my surprise, she turned to those in front of us and said, "It's the holidays, let's let this beautiful young lady go ahead because she's not feeling well." I'm sure because of her fame, they obliged. I'm not one to ask for help, but at that moment I was so humbled by her kindness.

That night it got to me. I broke down and sobbed. All I wanted was to get on my knees and pray, but I knew it would be impossible to get down and then back up. I thought I was being punished. I thought I would be crippled. I laid in my bed and looked up to God: "If this is your will, I will accept it." I would become a disabled person and rely on a wheelchair for the rest of my life.

I cried myself to sleep.

IT WAS TRADITION FOR ME TO COOK CHRISTMAS DINNER. Dre and my friends Marva and her husband Brian would be joining me. Finally, something to look forward to. We'd always have a feast and I would always have it ready by about 11am Christmas morning. But not this year. I couldn't stand for more than a few minutes without wincing in pain. I sat down in my director's chair and slowly prepared each dish. Everything took significantly longer than normal, but we were going to enjoy our meal together, whether I was on my feet or confined to a chair.

It may have been eight hours late, but I put a beautiful Christmas spread on the table for my son and guests. No one can say Cheyenne Martin doesn't persevere!

My doctor continued to give me Synvisc shots in my knees. It helped, but we realized it wasn't really what I needed. He was treating me for lost cartilage in my knees, but that wasn't the problem. Neither of us knew that at the time. Neither of us knew what was wrong with me. Our last visit in January he finally said, "I don't understand why your knees aren't getting better and why it's spread to other parts of your body." He thought perhaps I had lupus[1] and even suggested a few other diseases, including fibromyalgia[2], which frightened me. He even had me get an MRI of my knee to see if that could help determine what was going on. It's one thing to know something is seriously wrong with you, but to have no idea what it is, what sort of treatment is necessary or even available, if it's covered by insurance and if not, how much would it cost? And then what if it's life-threatening? This was almost too much for me to endure.

Being unsure of what was happening to me, my stress level increased exponentially. Continued high levels of stress will take its toll on your body and can make an otherwise healthy person sick. It can also make you look old beyond your years. Look at some of our past U.S. presidents. Bill Clinton and Barack Obama began their terms with their natural color hair, but by the end of their presidencies, both had noticeably grayer hair, more so with Clinton, but Obama definitely showed signs of aging as well. A direct result of stress, and I had to get mine under control.

I had just started my production company Emerald City Entertainment and set up an office in Sherman Oaks. By this time, I'd begun walking with a crutch and, despite the difficulties I was experiencing, I was determined to keep working and moving forward.

My doctor suggested I make an appointment with a rheumatologist. I was more than willing, but I had no idea what a rheumatologist even was or what they treated. I never even heard of a rheumatologist, so I did some research to learn as much as I could.

In February of 2016, I finally saw a rheumatologist, Dr. Adam Kreitenberg. This was almost a year from when I first noticed something was wrong. When I arrived, I was in really bad shape. He performed a great deal of different blood tests. I had to wait for about two weeks to get the results and that's when he broke the news.

I had very high levels of rheumatoid arthritis.

At long last, I finally knew what was happening to my body. Now it was time to determine the treatment. And I was ready to take on RA with all my might!

[1]*Lupus* *is a long-term autoimmune disease in which the body's immune system becomes hyperactive and attacks normal, healthy tissue. Symptoms include inflammation, swelling, and damage to the joints, skin, kidneys, blood, heart, and lungs. (Source: WebMD)*

[2]*Fibromyalgia* *is a disorder characterized by widespread musculoskeletal pain accompanied by fatigue, sleep, memory and mood issues. Researchers believe that fibromyalgia amplifies painful sensations by affecting the way your brain processes pain signals. (Source: WebMD)*

After a year of hell. A year of pain.

A year of not knowing what was going on.

Finally. I had the answer.

FOUR

A Sense of Relief?

I WAS RELIEVED. At least I knew what it was. I had one of many known autoimmune diseases. Now I knew what was wrong with me.

I had rheumatoid arthritis (RA).

I was very scared. Like most people, I immediately sought the advice once again of Dr. Google. I found pictures of people with deformed hands, fingers, ankles, knees; "Oh my God, was this my future?" My sense of relief quickly transformed into a sense of fear and anxiety; a sense of the unknown.

My doctor tried to put me at ease. "We have a relationship now. We're in this together." And that's when I started taking the meds. His first step was to prescribe methotrexate[1], which is used to treat cancer, psoriasis and of course RA. I was optimistic. But that optimism was put on hold when my doctor informed me it would take up to three months to take effect. I didn't understand why it would take so long. I wanted relief now! My doctor explained methotrexate is in a class of medications called Disease Modifying Anti-Rheumatic Drugs, or DMARDs. DMARDs are a slow acting, but a very effective treatment for RA. It's also considered the "gold standard" first line treatment for RA because of its effectiveness and side effect profile.

I guess I was just going to have to wait.

At my next appointment, I was told my insurance would not cover it and I was only allowed to see the rheumatologist every three months. His office assistant Sophia recommended an insurance broker who helped me find truly good insurance to cover the treatments and medications I needed.

IN EARLY MAY, RIGHT AROUND MY BIRTHDAY, I had a Jacuzzi installed in my backyard. I'd been told it was great for a person with RA. And it was! The heat from the water really made a difference.

Because it would take a while for the drugs to become effective, things were going to get worse, before they got better.

In my master bathroom, I have a circular whirlpool tub., which is fantastic for the RA as well. This one time I took a bath, drained the water and realized I couldn't get out of the bathtub! I tried to get on my knees, but that was too painful. I was stuck. I didn't know what to do. I became frightened. I hadn't brought my phone in with me, so I couldn't call for help and if I did, someone was going to see me stuck and naked in my tub.

What was I going to do?

It had been over thirty minutes now since I drained the water. I was cold and on the verge of a panic attack! Finally, and with a great deal of effort, I grabbed the faucet, pulled myself up, leaned onto the side of the tub, laid sideways and rolled over and out. I'm glad no one was there to see that. It seems almost comical now, but at the time it was humiliating. I felt so helpless.

My doctor had also prescribed the steroid prednisone[2], which would help reduce swelling and ibuprofen[3] (the main ingredient in Advil) for the pain. And I needed that. The pain was intense. As much good as a drug like ibuprofen can do, it also has nasty side effects. It can raise your blood pressure and cause ulcers, bleeding, and holes in your stomach and intestines.

I'd been taking all three meds for a few months and was finally starting to feel the results. I was able to move better with less pain. My knees were still swollen, my hands and fingers were puffy, and my ankles would give me grief once in a while. But it was so much easier to deal with than it had been. And I had a process. I'd wake up at 5am, take the (3) prednisone and (1) 400 mg of ibuprofen and go back to bed for about two hours. That way, they'd kick in when it was time for me to get up. I'd slip into a hot bath, soothe the joints and muscles, get ready for work and start my day. Come Saturday, I'd take my weekly dose of (8) methotrexate.

All drugs of this nature have side effects. And high blood pressure wasn't the only one I had to worry about.

One morning I was washing my hair when a small clump came loose into my hand. "I'm losing my hair now, too?!?!" I looked in the mirror. My hair was falling out, and I'd gained a lot of weight. I didn't like what I saw; it was rather frightening. My hair was noticeably thinner and it continued to fall out.

I've always enjoyed wearing weaves and wigs now and again to give my hair a fuller look or for a special occasion. I was wondering if I was going to have to wear them now because I had no choice.

I'm a young woman who should have plenty of life ahead of me. I've been diagnosed with an incurable autoimmune disease, I've gained a significant amount of weight, and my hair was falling out.

What else could go wrong?

My sister Tiffany wanted my nine-year-old niece Taylor to come visit for the summer. I was a little skeptical because I knew I was physically limited, but I agreed and she came to visit in early June.

Shortly after she arrived, we were in my bathroom and she said, "Aunt Cheyenne, you're chubby." "You think I'm fat?" She replied, "No, just chubby." I was thinking to myself, "I have gained weight."

Then the most embarrassing thing happened.

Taylor walked into my bathroom and saw my "process" to get out of the tub. "You do all of that to get out of the tub?" I scolded her and told her to get out of my bathroom! My embarrassment became anger. I felt helpless once again.

Nonetheless, we had a great summer together. We were very active and I couldn't believe that I was getting around as well as I was. We went horseback riding, fishing, rented a boat, spent a weekend at the Beverly Hills Hotel and flew to Vegas for the weekend. We were having a blast.

But I was gaining weight by the days. Taylor and I were eating well. She'd even gained weight, herself. Now she was chubby and I was fat. How depressing.

I finally had my sister Tiffany fly out for a week to join us. When I picked her up from the airport, she was giving me a strange look. I could tell she was taken aback by the weight I had gained.

Shortly after, Taylor was getting on my nerves and when I went to give her a piece of my mind, she ran down my hallway and I chased after her. I was amazed; me running? And so were Taylor and her mom; they both said: "You ran?" I was ecstatic! "I ran!"

At that very moment, I knew the Methotrexate had finally kicked in.

ONCE TIFFANY AND TAYLOR WENT back to Pittsburgh in the middle of August, I was on a serious mission to lose weight and get off the prednisone. I knew it was the cause of my weight gain.

I went cold turkey. Didn't even discuss it with my doctor.

He scolded me for making decisions about my medication without consulting him first. I just knew I had to stop taking that steroid.

Second step was to lose weight.

On September 15th I went to the weight loss clinic, Lindora. After I joined, I asked my house keeper to clean out my cupboards and refrigerator. All the bad food, snacks, red meat, cereal, bread—it all had to go.

November rolled around and I lost about fifteen pounds. I was beginning to feel like my old self. I was walking, running and I started to look good. I was still dealing with some small issues from the RA, but it was time for me to head to Pittsburgh for the second annual Turkey Drive for my charity, the Cheyenne Martin Foundation[4].

Giving back is extremely important to me, no matter how I feel. I had two hundred and fifty turkeys to hand out and a raffle for a free flat screen TV. I wasn't going to let the community down.

The Turkey Drive was a success; I made it through with no issues. I sat down every chance I could, but no one was the wiser, nor did they have any idea what was going on with me.

[1]*Methotrexate* is used to treat certain types of cancer or to control severe psoriasis or rheumatoid arthritis that has not responded to other treatments. Methotrexate belongs to a class of drugs known as antimetabolites. It works by slowing or stopping the growth of cancer cells and suppressing the immune system.

Early treatment of rheumatoid arthritis with more aggressive therapy such as Methotrexate helps to reduce further joint damage and to preserve joint function. (Source: WebMD)

[2]*Prednisone* is used to treat conditions such as arthritis, blood disorders, breathing problems, severe allergies, skin diseases, cancer, eye problems, and immune system disorders. Prednisone belongs to a class of drugs known as corticosteroids. It decreases your immune system's response to various diseases to reduce symptoms such as swelling and allergic-type reactions. (Source: WebMD)

[3]*Ibuprofen* is used to relieve pain from various conditions such as headache, dental pain, menstrual cramps, muscle aches, or arthritis. It is also used to reduce fever and to relieve minor aches and pain due to the common cold or flu. Ibuprofen is a nonsteroidal anti-inflammatory drug (NSAID). It works by blocking your body's production of certain natural substances that cause inflammation. This effect helps to decrease swelling, pain, or fever. (Source: WebMD)

[4]*Cheyenne Martin Foundation (CMF)* Founded in 2015 by Cheyenne Martin, is a recognized nonprofit organization serving underserved and underrepresented communities throughout the Los Angeles and Pittsburgh areas. Dedicated to impacting the lives of women disadvantaged by social or economic circumstances, CMF works locally and nationally to shine a light on women experiencing hardships. As advocates, we believe the basic human right for all people to have peace of mind, food to nourish their bodies and a safe place to sleep at night. https://www.cheyennemartinfoundation.org

We have choices in life.

We can sit around, feel sorry for ourselves
and just accept what cards we're dealt.
Or we can decide to make a change.

I made a lot of changes. I had to.

FIVE

From Good To Bad; From Bad To Worse

MY DOCTOR TOLD ME I WAS A SUCCESS STORY. My blood work came back positive and my inflammation numbers were lower. So many women would come to him diagnosed with RA and completely ignore what he suggested they do to battle it. They wouldn't change their diet, they wouldn't change their lifestyle, and they would return to him in pain—time and time again.

That wasn't going to be me.

After going to Lindora to lose weight, I made some big changes. First was sugar. Refined sugar is in so much of our food, especially processed foods. And it's so very bad for you. Second was red meat. Sugar and red meat are the enemy of someone with RA.

Goodbye sugar! Goodbye red meat!

I continued my treatment at Lindora. Three times a week I had to urinate on a stick and if it turned purple, that meant I was in ketosis[1] and losing weight. Twice a week I would get vitamin B12[2] and lipotropic[3] shots, which also helped with weight loss, mental clarity and improving my energy levels.

Christmas 2016 was good. I still missed Marqese. It was my second Christmas without him; I was feeling better overall, but it was still difficult to move on. As time passed, I would remember the good and much less of the bad. I think we all like to see the good in everyone, despite their flaws.

Come January 2017, I'd lost twenty-five pounds. I was proud of that.

I started focusing on a film project, which was exciting. But my left elbow started acting up. It just wasn't cooperating. I could only extend it about two-thirds of normal compared to my right. It was achy, uncomfortable and I was irritated it wasn't working properly.

Time to visit the doctor.

He gave me a cortisone[4] shot in my elbow, which helped quite a bit—not only with reducing the pain, but with mobility. Of course when you improve one thing, something else has to come up. My left knee was beginning to give me trouble again. Nothing like before, but it was slightly swollen and causing me discomfort. My doctor suggested I start a regimen of the biologic[5] etanercept[6] (also known as Enbrel[7]), which would help reduce inflammation. They use this to treat psoriasis and other forms of arthritis as well.

I would administer this myself with weekly shots into my stomach. And they weren't cheap. Fortunately, my insurance did cover them or I would've been out of pocket $500 per shot, per week!

Every Wednesday, I'd pull up my shirt and alternate injecting myself two fingers' space on either side of my belly button. Switching sides helped prevent bruising. The swelling went down. I felt amazing. Everything was going great!

But it was too good to be true.

IN FEBRUARY, RIGHT BEFORE VALENTINE'S DAY, I was working at my office and got up to get some water. I headed down the hall and suddenly became very disoriented. I was light-headed and thought I was going to faint. I figured I just needed some water and would be okay. After about five minutes I felt better. It scared me, but being my optimistic self, I figured it was just a fluke.

About a week later, I noticed other things were changing. My swelling was down, but something wasn't right. I'd wake up in the middle of the night and found I had been scratching myself in the groin. Maybe I was dreaming. So I reviewed my surveillance footage and sure enough, I was vigorously scratching myself! I freaked out. Even though I wasn't sexually active at the time, I thought I'd contracted an STD, perhaps crabs.

I went to the store and got the crabs medicine. I starting regularly applying it and kept looking for them, but nothing was there. "Why was I scratching myself? What's happening to me now?" It was so bad.

And then the disorientation returned.

I'd been out with a friend and when I returned home, it happened. I became light-headed and disoriented all over again. The anxiety was overwhelming. I took a hot bath to hopefully calm my nerves and return to normal. After my bath I laid down. It took a short while but I did feel better.

Meanwhile, I was starting to rapidly lose weight, and not in a good way. Friends started to notice. Certainly I wanted to lose the weight I had gained, but not in an unhealthy or dangerous way.

But that wasn't all that was changing.

I went to get a mani-pedi and while the technician was working on my feet, I noticed there was a small pale patch of skin. I actually told her not to scrub so hard, thinking it was removing pigment somehow. I looked like I had vitiligo (the condition that causes patches of skin to lose their pigment). I figured this too was a fluke and it would go away.

I was once again wrong.

The pale patch continued to get bigger and bigger, to about the diameter of a small tangerine. Then on the bottom of my feet I developed these itchy red bumps. And if that wasn't enough, my eye sight was becoming blurry.

Off to the doctor I went.

He told me that the etanercept shots can have kooky side effects. "Kooky side effects?" He was right about that. Spells of disorientation; itching and scratching myself. Pigment loss on my skin and red, sore patches on the bottom of my feet. I also became increasingly sensitive to the flavor of food. Everything tasted way too salty. What else could go wrong? Enough!

I continued with the weekly shots because it was really helping my RA.

I was still losing weight when I went to see my acupuncture doctor, Dr. Ho. He looked at me with wide eyes, "Oh my goodness Cheyenne, you've lost too much weight!" I didn't know how to react. One thing after another kept going wrong. It was upsetting. I was always on edge.

IT WAS TIME TO CELEBRATE MY BIRTHDAY. That should make me feel better. I was optimistic.

My girlfriend Ky took me out for some Japanese food. We were having a nice time, but of course she had to tell them it was my special day. They snuck up behind me and burst out with "Happy Birthday to You!" I was startled like never before. I practically jumped out of my seat! Ky asked me what was wrong. I told her they just caught me off guard. But it was like I was super sensitive to sound. I felt like I could hear everyone's conversation in the restaurant. Everything seemed really loud and intense. I needed to go home and go to bed.

I stayed home from work the next day. My anxiety was horrible and I needed to just chill.

Later, my girlfriend Kieren called and said she had tickets to see Stevie Wonder that night. That actually sounded great. I could relax and enjoy some good music. Hopefully the sounds wouldn't bother me.

It took me four hours to get dressed. The anxiety would kick in just as I entered a room and I'd walk right back out. It was ridiculous! I kept hearing things. Weird sounds. I walked into my dressing room and it sounded like about twenty crickets were in there. And it seemed like they were following me from room to room. I thought I was going crazy. This concert would be a good distraction.

I called my driver to take me to pick up Kieren. With everything going on, there was no way I could drive myself.

My driver arrived and we were on our way. He chatted with me until we made it to the address I'd given him. He pulled over, stopped and said for me to tell Kieren to come out. But nothing looked familiar. I asked if he took me to the right address. "This is the address you entered." The address was correct, but the surroundings were not. I didn't recognize anything. I was staring at Kieren's house and it was like I'd never seen it before. After a moment I was nearly hysterical and I asked him to just take me back home.

I got home, knelt down and began to pray. Something was horribly wrong.

In the morning, I took an Uber to see my doctor. My driver wasn't available and I still wasn't comfortable driving. I'd looked and felt horrible. He asked if I was okay. I was not. I told him about my disorientation spells. Places I'd driven to for years required me using my GPS, even if it was close by. My go-to grocery store where I knew where everything was, was now completely unfamiliar. I had lost my memory. I couldn't remember anything. I was so afraid.

I thought I was dying. The doctor assured me I was not, and to be patient, as it would take time for me to adjust to the meds.

I was still hyper-sensitive to noise. Every little sound would affect me. And I'd keep hearing this high-pitched ringing in my ears. I would shut off my phones. I didn't want to hear from anyone. The only things I could tolerate watching on television were comedies or something uplifting.

I think I must've watched the movie *Splash* over fifty times.

IT WAS A MONDAY IN MAY AND THESE ANXIETY-FUELED SPELLS WERE OUT OF CONTROL. I constantly felt faint, out of my wits and out of control. Finally, I called my friend Elicia to take me to the ER. When we arrived, I was so pale they actually listed my race as white, if you can believe that. They put me on an IV. I started to feel better and eventually they sent me home.

Elicia dropped me off and I went inside to take another bath. The bath became my safe place. It's where I felt most comfortable. Only this time I started shaking and I didn't feel safe. I had the chills, but it was May. And May in Los Angeles is not the least bit cold. The following morning, I woke up with very bad pains in my stomach. It was like someone was twisting my intestines tighter and tighter. After a few hours it seemed to have stopped.

I just couldn't keep food down during this time, either, which was probably a factor in the weight loss.

Come Friday night my heart was beating so fast, I thought it was going to jump out of my chest. I was back at the ER. "What's wrong with me? Am I having a heart attack?" They ran various tests including an EKG and blood work. I was frantic. They finally put me in a room. The hospital sounds were too much. All the beeping and tones they make; the old woman moaning nearby; the old man crying out for his meds. All I could do was shake. My heart was racing. My mind was racing. "Should I just write a will right now?" I didn't think I would make it out alive. On top of everything else, no one knew I was at the hospital. I had to keep this to myself.

The doctor came in and said after running fifteen tests, they couldn't find anything wrong. He said perhaps they could run a brain MRI, but he didn't think that was the issue. I told him about my disorientation and he suggested I go back to my regular doctor. After keeping me there all night, they finally discharged me at 8:30am.

I arrived home and was greeted by my housekeeper, who looked at me with concern. I was skinny from my weight loss and just didn't look like myself. I looked frail. "Miss Cheyenne, why don't you just lie down and let me know if you need anything." I dozed off for about fifteen minutes or so and when I woke up, I didn't recognize her or know where I was. It took a minute or so for me to regain my composure.

I had enough of this ongoing and debilitating brain fog.

At first I planned to go back to the ER, but I waited. I ended up talking with my friend Nancy, who was the office manager where I received physical therapy, about what had been happening and she suggested I see Dr. Craig Jace who practiced holistic eastern medicine, something she whole-heartedly supported. I figured I had nothing to lose. I called to make an appointment and they said I had to wait two weeks. I couldn't wait two weeks! I finally convinced them to see me right away.

When I got in to see the doctor, he had blood drawn and we talked. I told him about all of the problems I'd been having, especially the disorientation. Then I explained what meds I was taking.

After a week, I returned to his office to go over the test results. He said because of my weakened immune system, which is a direct result of the methotrexate and etanercept, I had developed candidiasis[8], an overgrowth of the fungus candida[9] within my body.

Here we go again!

[1]*Ketosis is a normal metabolic process, something your body does to keep working. When it doesn't have enough carbohydrates from food for your cells to burn for energy, it burns fat instead. As part of this process, it makes ketones. (Source: WebMD)*

[2]*B12 or Cyanocobalamin is a man-made form of vitamin B12 used to treat low levels (deficiency) of this vitamin. Vitamin B12 helps your body use fat and carbohydrates for energy and make new protein. It is also important for normal blood, cells, and nerves. Most people get enough vitamin B12 in their diet, but a deficiency may occur in certain health conditions (e.g., poor nutrition, stomach/intestinal problems, infection, cancer). Serious vitamin B12 deficiency may result in anemia, stomach problems, and nerve damage. (Source: WebMD)*

[3]*Lipotropic injections are typically offered by weight loss clinics and medispas who create unique compounds that they sell as lipo injections. Even though different clinics have different formulas, there are a few ingredients that are fairly standard: Vitamin B12; Methionine: An essential amino acid that plays an important role in metabolism; Inositol: A vitamin-like natural sugar related to the B vitamin family. Inositol helps to metabolize fat and may improve insulin function in the body; And Choline: An essential nutrient that is related to the B vitamins. It is responsible for lipid (fat) metabolism and transport and has other jobs in the body related to cell membrane structure and other functions. (Source: VeryWellFit)*

[4]*Cortisone is a pregnane steroid hormone. (Source: WikiPedia); Cortisone injections can be used to treat inflammation of small areas of the body, such as inflammation of a specific joint or tendon. They can also treat inflammation that is widespread throughout the body, such as with allergic reactions, asthma, and rheumatoid arthritis, which affects many joints. (Source: WedMD)*

[5]*A biologic drug is a product that is produced from living organisms or contain components of living organisms. Biologics include recombinant proteins, tissues, genes, allergens, cells, blood components, blood, and vaccines. Biologics are used to treat numerous disease and conditions. (Source: Medicine Net)*

[6]*Etanercept Subcutaneous sold as the brand [7]Enbrel is used alone or in combination with an immunosuppressant (such as*

Methotrexate) to treat certain types of arthritis (such as rheumatoid, psoriatic, juvenile idiopathic, and ankylosing spondylitis). etanercept controls your body's defensive response by blocking the action of a certain natural substance (TNF) that is used by the immune system. Treatment decreases the pain, swelling and stiffness of joints in arthritis. This medication can stop the progression of disease and joint damage, resulting in improved daily functioning and quality of life.

This medication treats but does not cure autoimmune diseases. Symptoms usually return within 1 month of stopping the medication. *(Source: WedMD)*

[8]Candidiasis *is a fungal infection caused by yeasts that belong to the genus* **[9]Candida.** *There are over 20 species of Candida yeasts that can cause infection in humans, the most common of which is Candida albicans. Candida yeasts normally reside in the intestinal tract and can be found on mucous membranes and skin without causing infection; however, overgrowth of these organisms can cause symptoms to develop. Symptoms of candidiasis vary depending on the area of the body that is infected. (Source: Center for Disease Control and Prevention)*

Cheyenne at 6 years old living with her paternal grandmother Mary Martin on a farm in Oregon.

Cheyenne and niece Taylor having fun in Las Vegas.

Cheyenne with her son Dre at his high school graduation.

Boxing has always been her passion, even after RA.

Center & Bottom: On vacation in Cabo San Lucas, Mexico.

Left: Cheyenne with entrepreneur and close friend, Chastity Clark.

Taking her horse Princess Dandy for a ride.

Nothing like a round of golf on a warm day.

Hitting the slopes in Big Bear, CA.

Snow mobiling after some screenings at the Sundance Film Festival in Park City, Utah

Investor meeting at the Versace mansion.

Opposite page: Grabbing the bull by the… horns in New York!

In 2017 Cheyenne and The Cheyenne Martin Foundation were in honored by the City of Los Angeles with Certificates of Recognition for her support, dedication and commitment to the Watts community.

From left: Andre Bowie, Darnell Clark, Destiny Medina, Mary Nesby, Cheyenne Martin and Sweetie Sherrie at the 2018 Cheyenne Martin Foundation Turkey Drive in Pittsburgh.

On the red carpet for the premiere of Disney's Big Hero 6 with famed writer, Peter Allen.

Getting some work done at the Emerald City Entertainment offices.

From left: Cheyenne's Mother Wanda Bowie, Grandmother Iola Bowie and Cheyenne on the purple carpet for the 2018 Cheyenne Martin Foundation Turkey Drive in Pittsburgh.

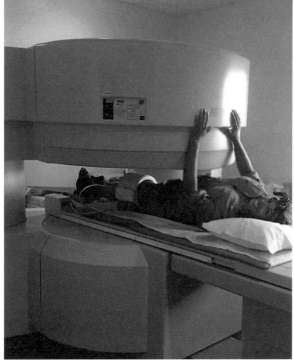

Pre-RA diagnosis knee MRI.

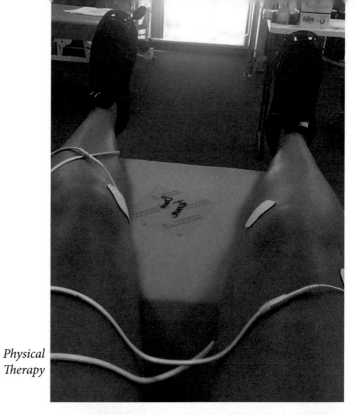

Physical Therapy

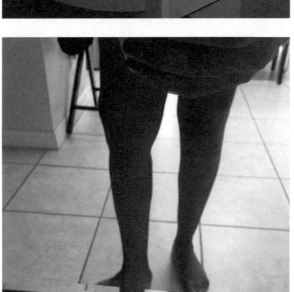

Synvisc Injections

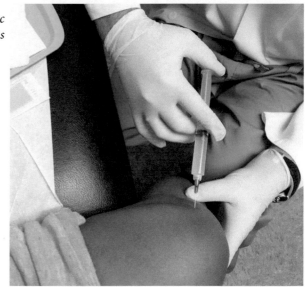

Acupuncture Treatment

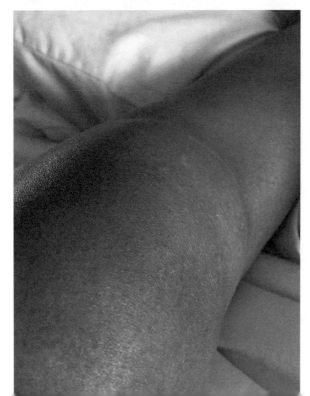

Middle & Bottom Left: Closeups of the major swelling of Cheyenne's knee from RA.

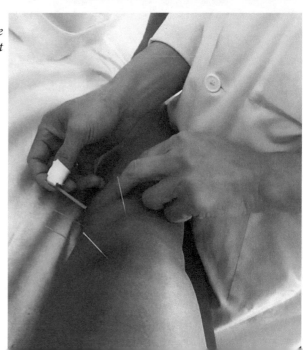

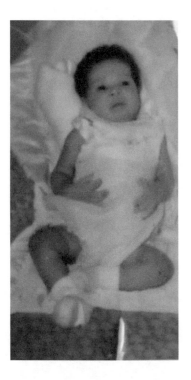

Clockwise: Baby girl, Alpha-Female, Boarding a private jet to Vegas and on the set of Wild'n Out with friend Jason Lee.

It all starts with the gut.
If your gut is healthy…

You're healthy.

SIX

One Thing Leads To Another

MUCH LIKE MY MYSTERY ILLNESS was determined to be RA, now I knew what was causing my brain fog and other problems. As they say, if it's not one thing, it's another. My RA was under control and that part of my life was pretty good. But this brain fog, the pigment discoloration on my left foot, the tiny red bumps that were underneath it, and everything else was just plain messing with me.

Dr. Jace discovered I had a candida overgrowth. Which is a naturally occurring fungus within the body. Under normal circumstances it isn't a problem, but because my immune system was compromised from the RA drugs, I now had to deal with that as well as a hormone imbalance, magnesium deficiency and hypothyroidism[1] (an underactive thyroid). The thyroid gland produces hormones that affect the heart, brain, muscles, skin—pretty much every part of the body—and mine wasn't working properly.

He put me on a three-month candida cleanse with a very restrictive diet. I could NOT have: sugar or artificial sweeteners, starchy vegetables (potatoes, corn, squash, peas), high-sugar fruits (bananas, raisins, grapes), milk, cheese, most bread, red meat, refined oils, caffeine or alcohol.

Most of it was easy to give up. Most of it!

What I COULD have included: low-sugar fruits in small amounts (lemons, limes, berries), non-starchy vegetables (asparagus, brussels sprouts, cabbage, broccoli, kale, celery, cucumber, eggplant, onion, spinach, zucchini, tomatoes); and I love my asparagus! I could also have: high-quality protein, which included salmon. I love my salmon, too! So this was a good thing. Herbal teas, herbs and spices, healthy fats (avocados, unrefined coconut oil, extra virgin olive oil, sesame oil) and gluten-free grains like quinoa were okay as well.

At first it seemed complex, but once I got accustomed to it, it wasn't really all that bad. If it was going to improve my health, then that's what I was going to do.

Dr. Jace and I were fairly certain all of my new symptoms were caused by the etanercept (aka Enbrel). I'd been on the methotrexate for over a year with minimal side affects. But once I started the etanercept and its effects kicked in, my symptoms began. Methotrexate is an anti-inflammatory, but also a mild immunosuppressant[2].

Essentially I was taking two immunosuppressants and that was the problem.

Dr. Jace suggested I stop taking the etanercept. To be honest, I had already stopped about a week prior. I'm fairly certain I was supposed to ween myself off the etanercept, but I didn't care and I stopped. Although it would be a while before the side effects subsided, this was a step in the right direction.

Dr. Jace also prescribed some natural fungal supplements called Fungal DX and Fungal Assist, which helped with the candida issue. What impressed me the most is that he was having me treat my symptoms by changing my diet. I was beginning to learn that it all starts with the gut. A healthy gut means a healthy person.

On the weekends, he had me try taking Nystatin[3] to help stop the fungus growth. If it didn't bother my stomach or cause me any discomfort, then I should continue with it. He was determined to get my candida under control and the Nystatin didn't seem to be a problem.

It was difficult at first with the restricted diet and regimen, but anyone who knows me, knows if I commit to something, there's no stopping me. I didn't give in to any temptation whatsoever. If I went out to eat with friends, I stuck to my diet. And fast food wasn't even an option.

THIS WHOLE EXPERIENCE WITH THE CANDIDA OVERGROWTH WAS WORSE THAN THE RA. The RA attacked my joints and caused swelling and what not, but that was under control. This brain fog and the other symptoms were attacking all of me—attacking my being.

After about two weeks, I started noticing a big difference. The pigment discoloration on my foot was getting smaller. My head was clear and my memory was coming back. I was still dealing with the anxiety and I wasn't one hundred percent comfortable driving, so I had my driver take me around for a few more weeks.

As I progressed with this new treatment, my RA doctor told me to watch out for holistic doctors. He told me they always blame these symptoms on candida. I told him the proof is in the results. I was feeling better and my symptoms where going away. You can't argue with that.

I was most definitely getting better, but I wasn't out of the woods just yet.

THAT JUNE, producer Will Packer *(Straight Outta Compton, What Men Want)* was having a private screening of his new film (at the time) *Girls Trip* at Creative Artists Agency (CAA) in Century City (next door to Beverly Hills), and a friend invited me to be her guest. This would be a great networking opportunity and since I was on the mend, I eagerly accepted the invitation.

When I arrived, it was a Hollywood Who's Who: producers, executive producers, agents, managers, famous and up-and-coming actors. There was an energetic buzz in the air.

And once again it was as if I could hear everyone's conversations. It was all around me. It was deafening. I wanted to network and meet people, but it was too much.

I excused myself to the adjacent courtyard to get some air. I took a deep breath and thought: "You know what this is. Just go back inside and block out those sounds. Start networking! These are your peers, these are people you'd like to work with, you have to do this!" I took another couple deep breaths, pulled myself together and headed back in.

I enjoyed the film and afterwards, a friend introduced me to Packer and his producing partner from Rainforest Films, James Lopez *(About Last Night, Think Like A Man)*. I was very glad to meet them and others I met at the event. It was tough, and I had to keep reminding myself, "You know what's wrong, and you can deal with it." And I did. I was proud of myself.

Soon after, I had an event of my own to attend. It was the Summer Women's Luncheon sponsored by my charity, The Cheyenne Martin Foundation. This event was to benefit underprivileged women, homeless, survivors of domestic abuse; anyone who needed help. I enlisted the help of a few of my celebrity friends and together we prepared lunch for one hundred and twenty-five women.

It touched my heart when one of the women from the shelter came up to me: "We full today, we even could go back for seconds." Hearing something like that makes it all worthwhile. Our goal was to empower these women to get back on their feet and overcome adversity.

No matter how much success might come my way, it's always incredibly important for me to give back. The event was a huge success, even though I still had some anxiety, because these events can be overwhelming. I made it through like a champ!

COME AUGUST, I'D COMPLETED MY CANDIDA CLEANSE and my fungus levels were where they should be. I was looking and feeling great. I was off the supplements, but pretty much stuck to my new diet. My RA was under control. No more brain fog, no confusion and my hair started growing back! I was really beginning to feel like myself again. I was even able to start exercising and playing golf again. The only issue was a strange gurgling in my stomach every once in a while, especially after I ate. And it started to get worse. In fact, one day I ended up literally vomiting all over myself while driving.

When will the problems end?

I contacted Dr. Jace and told him what was happening. He suspected a magnesium deficiency and told me to pick up some magnesium floradix, an over-the-counter liquid mineral supplement. He also suggested I try G.I. Benefits by DaVinci Laboratories, which is a natural digestive aid to help support gut health, and soothe the digestive tract. It's supposed to help with regularity and microbial balance, and supports proper immune function.

It didn't work for me. My stomach was still acting up.

I went to see Dr. Kreitenberg, my RA doctor, and he recommended I see a gastroenterologist[4]. So I did. He gave me a test to see if I had the bacteria, H. Pylori[5]. I did not. Then what was causing all these stomach problems?

Since I'd been feeling better, I did start to eat foods that weren't on my restricted diet and perhaps that's what caused the digestive issues. Dr. Jace said he felt I should re-introduce these foods very slowly to allow my body to adjust. In hindsight, I think I started up on other foods too quickly.

I followed Dr. Jace's advice and also began taking simple digestive supplements along with meals, which helped settle my stomach problems.

IN THE FALL OF 2017, THINGS WERE ON THE UPSWING YET AGAIN. RA wasn't bothering me and I was looking forward to the holidays. This year, I had my charity's Turkey Drive in California and gave away two hundred and fifty turkeys to the underprivileged in South Central Los Angeles. All went well.

Christmas was great. I was happy. I was in the best health I'd been in years. My weight was good. I was starting to feel good about life, minus the stomach gurgling, although it was happening less. I started seeing someone. I got involved in a relationship that unfortunately became dysfunctional. This brought on a lot of stress in a very short time. I did not want to go down that road again. Nonetheless, I kept a smile on my face as 2018 looked very promising.

In February, I had ended that unhealthy relationship. I decided to head to New York for business and to spend some time with my good friend Jason Lee. He invited me to visit him on the set of MTV's *Wild 'N Out*. While I was there, I met a driver who was very kind and engaging. As we chatted, I told him I worked in the entertainment business and about my foundation that caters to women's empowerment. He was intrigued and later introduced me to one of his clients.

We met and she was impressed with the work that I was doing with my foundation and film company. We really hit it off. Since then, she has been instrumental in opening several doors for me and has inspired me to become a better business-woman.

It goes to show you never know who you'll meet or who they might be associated with. Just a simple conversation with that caring man in the car made for a life-changing trip.

It was very, very cold in New York at that time and I was concerned my RA could've been a problem, but it wasn't. All was good.

IN MARCH, the new investor I met in New York wanted me to meet one of her investor colleagues in Miami. Off to Florida I went. Everything was going well. Friday night, we had a business meeting at the Versace mansion. I was excited about finally getting the chance to see this amazing place. The food, the environment, it was five stars all the way. On Saturday, our dinner meeting was planned for the investor's home on Star Island.

I was getting ready for the meeting in my hotel room, looked in the mirror and thought I was looking sharp. I grabbed my iPhone to take some selfies. I rotated my leg to pose and then I felt it. I knew I'd done something. My knee began to rapidly swell. It was like the beginnings of RA all over again. What did I do?

My knee was now the size of a small balloon. Not this again!

[1]**Hypothyroidism**, *also called underactive thyroid disease, is a common disorder. With hypothyroidism, your thyroid gland does not make enough thyroid hormone. The thyroid gland is located in the front lower part of your neck. Hormones released by the gland travel through your bloodstream and affect nearly every part of your body, from your heart and brain, to your muscles and skin. (Source: WebMD)*

[2]**Immunosuppressants** *are drugs that inhibit or prevent activity of the immune system.*

[3]**Nystatin** *is used to treat fungal infections of the inside of the mouth and lining of the stomach and intestines. Nystatin is in a class of antifungal medications called polyenes. It works by stopping the growth of fungi that cause infection. (Source: MedLine Plus)*

[4]*A* **Gastroenterologist** *is a physician with dedicated training and unique experience in the management of diseases of the gastrointestinal tract and liver. (Source: American College of Gastroenterology)*

[5]**H. Pylori** *(Helicobacter pylori) is a type of bacteria. These germs can enter your body and live in your digestive tract. After many years, they can cause sores, called ulcers, in the lining of your stomach or the upper part of your small intestine. (Source: WebMD)*

Change is hard. Change is difficult.
Change is even frustrating.

But changing bad habits and one's lifestyle
has amazing results.

SEVEN

Back On My Feet

WHILE TAKING SEVERAL SELFIES, I somehow twisted my leg just so and made my RA come back with a vengeance! That'll teach me to be vain! I can laugh about it now, but not then. It was bad.

Despite being in pain, I made it to my investor dinner and all went quite well. I put on my best game face and they had no idea anything was wrong with me.

The next morning, I woke up in excruciating pain. The swelling hadn't gone down, it had increased. I made it to the beach to spend time with my good friend Sweetie, her daughter (my god daughter) and Sweetie's mother. I was hoping the warmth of the sun would help ease the pain. I ended up meeting this woman who said she was familiar with RA. We talked for a bit and she offered to massage it out so I'd look and feel better. She seemed smart and appeared to know what she was talking about, so I let her do her thing.

That was a big mistake.

I know she meant well, but she made it worse. Much worse! Before, it was the size of a small balloon; now it was as big as a watermelon! It was huge and I was miserable that evening!

I put on my trusty leg brace for the flight home. I'd worn the brace from time to time to ease the pain and help with mobility. Thank God I had it with me! And thank goodness I fly first class so there was plenty of room for me to stretch out and elevate my leg while heading back to LA.

Once I was home, I immediately made an appointment with Dr. Kreitenberg. First thing was a cortisone shot to the knee to ease the pain and reduce the swelling. He told me even though my RA had been under control, there would be the occasional flare-up, which is what happened in Miami. It can be brought on for a variety of reasons: stress, poor diet and apparently standing wrong while taking a selfie!

We talked about what to do when this happens. And he emphasized that it would happen again, but if I was prepared, it wouldn't necessarily be too bad. I needed to take it easy, keep the knee elevated and get plenty of rest.

Since I'd had my first flare-up, and there would certainly be more, he suggested I try the drug tofacitinib[1] (typically known as Xeljanz). Oh HELL no! After what happened with the etanercept, I wasn't having any of that. I was adamant!

The swelling on my knee did go down, but not all the way and it was still causing me a lot of discomfort. I had business to attend to in San Francisco so I just dealt with it the best I could.

NOW WE WERE INTO JUNE OF 2018 and I had a flare-up on my right wrist. It was from just below my fingers to the top of my forearm, where it became swollen and quite painful. I couldn't even sign my name to a check if I wanted to. I went back to Dr. Kreitenberg's office, but he was out, so I saw one of his colleagues who gave me a cortisone shot directly into my wrist. It definitely helped with the pain, and the swelling did go down. At this point, my knee was still a bit swollen and achy, too.

My foundation was sponsoring an event at Junior Achievement of Southern California (JASoCal)[2] near Burbank. I brought in sixty 14 to 18-year-old girls from all walks of life to be adults for the day. My knee was aching, but it was imperative I put on a brave face and be strong for my young girls.

This knee was working my last nerve.

Now that I was experiencing flare-ups, I wanted to treat them, but I didn't want to keep getting the cortisone shots, which were really just a temporary fix. I decided to see Dr. Blanton, an orthopedist I knew, to determine if Dr. Kreitenberg might have missed something.

I drove about an hour and twenty minutes to Riverside to see him. First step was to get some X-rays. Upon examination, he explained that the cartilage in my left knee had partial thickness loss, which is a symptom of osteoarthritis. This was a result of day-to-day wear and tear on my knee, not my RA. However, in some instances, RA can lead to osteoarthritis, because it attacks the joints, eventually causing damage.

To treat this, he said I should I start taking glucosamine sulfate[3] and turmeric[4] supplements, which would be a natural, organic means of reducing inflammation and help increase the mobility of my knee. I started taking both and continued taking ibuprofen as well for the pain.

He suggested the injection procedure PRP (platelet rich plasma)[6] therapy, which would use a component of my own blood to repair the damage to my knee joint. I was seriously considering it, but it would've required I stop taking ibuprofen for a week prior and I couldn't do that.
Actually I could have.

I later learned from Dr. Kreitenberg that the ibuprofen was to be taken as needed, not daily. And that prolonged use can cause damage to the lining of your stomach and lead to serious issues. Had I known this, I probably would've gone ahead with the PRP therapy, which at some point I may still have done in the future.

Once again things were going well. I'd been taking the glucosamine and turmeric and was feeling much better; I could even work out and exercise again. All good stuff. I was happy. That Thanksgiving I was back in Pittsburgh for my Turkey Drive and to meet with the Pittsburgh film office about my newest project, a television pilot.

That time of year in Da Burgh, as the locals call it, is freezing cold. But it didn't affect me in the least. This girl was on fire! I had a great deal of work to do with the Turkey Drive, which included a lot of walking. At one point I felt the beginnings of what could've become a nasty cold; I doubled up on the Vitamin C, and I was good as new.

The event was a success.

Christmas came and although I had a brief flare-up for a couple days, I handled it with no problem whatsoever and was back on my feet in no time.

I DID SOME MORE RESEARCH and started to include Lypo-Spheric™ Vitamin C[7] into my daily regimen. Even as kids, we know Vitamin C is good for us, but it's not nearly as effective taken like most people take it, because its benefits are destroyed during digestion before it can do any good. The Lypo-Spheric process allows for greater absorption into the bloodstream, making it far more effective. This is often prescribed to cancer patients and others with weakened immune systems and poor health. Even if you aren't in poor health, it's great to have Vitamin C daily in your body, keeping you strong.

During my research I discovered chicken can trigger mucous production and I wanted nothing to do with that. Whereas, salmon does the opposite and reduces it. I'd already given up red meat, so now it was time for a major decision.

I am going to be a pescatarian.

Which simply means I would have no meat other than fish and shell fish. The healthier my diet, the healthier I was. It all starts with what we put into our bodies.

Like most people though, I'd spent most of my life not eating as good as I should. Now that I'm pursuing a healthy lifestyle it was time for another big change.

Time to get years and years of built-up waste out of my body!

---

[1]*Tofacitinib (Xeljanz) is used to treat psoriatic arthritis and moderate-to-severe forms of rheumatoid arthritis. It helps to decrease pain/tenderness/swelling in the joints. (Source: WebMD)*

[2]*JASoCal's programs seek to inspire and empower young people through financial literacy, workforce readiness and entrepreneurship education; all concepts that are reinforced through JA's volunteer mentors who lead students through JA Classroom, Job Shadow and Finance Park programs.*

[3]*Glucosamine Sulfate is a naturally occurring chemical found in the human body. It is in the fluid that is around joints. (Source: WebMD)*

[4]*Turmeric and especially its most active compound Curcumin[5] have many scientifically-proven health benefits, such as the*

potential to prevent heart disease, Alzheimer's and cancer. It's a potent anti-inflammatory and antioxidant and may also help improve symptoms of depression and arthritis. (Source: HealthLine)

[5]***Curcumin*** *is strongly anti-inflammatory. In fact, it's so powerful that it matches the effectiveness of some anti-inflammatory drugs, without the side effects. (Source: HealthLine)*

[6]***Platelet-rich plasma*** *(PRP) therapy, uses injections of a concentration of a patient's own platelets to accelerate the healing of injured tendons, ligaments, muscles and joints. In this way, PRP injections use each individual patient's own healing system to improve musculoskeletal problems.*

PRP injections are prepared by taking anywhere from one to a few tubes of the patient's own blood and running it through a centrifuge to concentrate the platelets. The activated platelets are then injected directly into the injured or diseased body tissue, releasing growth factors that stimulate and increase the number of reparative cells. (Source: Hospital For Special Surgery)

[7]***Lypo-Spheric Vitamin C*** *uses liposomes (a tiny spherical sac of phospholipid molecules enclosing a water droplet, especially as formed artificially to carry drugs or other substances into the tissues.) to protect the active nutrients during digestion. This means more Vitamin C is absorbed by your cells with the nutrients still intact and ready to work. (Source: Family Health Diary)*

Western medicine practices the idea

of treating symptoms

and not preventing the cause.

That's just plain backwards thinking.

EIGHT

Cleansing the Mind, Body & Soul

OBVIOUSLY WE ALL KNOW there's big money to be made from prescribing overpriced drugs. But that doesn't mean we have to agree with it, or take part. I'm not saying all doctors and insurance companies are bad, but there is a great deal of misinformation and downright counter-productive practices going on every day. So many Americans are like sheep and just follow whatever their doctor tells them. They don't seek a second opinion or explore their options. When in fact, they could've easily done some research and found alternative treatments to prolong their life far longer than their doctor who's receiving kickbacks from Big Pharma.

It all starts with the gut.

It's estimated that ninety percent of diseases begin in the gut. It all starts with toxins. It all starts with taking care of yourself before there is a problem. Or in my case, when I learned I had RA. I took steps to keep it from getting worse. I started eating better. I found doctors who had my best interests at heart and I sought out treatment from a licensed colonic hydrotherapist.

Until recently, colonics were most often only used prior to a colonoscopy. Certainly that's a good means of preventive medicine, but you don't usually get your first colonoscopy until you're 45-50 years old and if there aren't any problems, not again for another 10 years. Why not get that poison and built-up waste out of your body on a more frequent basis? When toxins aren't present, the body is more efficient, which can prevent disease. It sounds overly simple, but it's true.

I'd rather take positive steps to prevent myself from getting sick, thank you very much!

I have had the pleasure of receiving and continue to receive on-going treatment from Karin Nahmani[1], a colonic hydrotherapist here in Los Angeles. She was kind enough to sit down with me for a chat about what she does and how it has benefited my on-going battle with RA. A battle that I am most definitely winning!

"When Cheyenne first came to me it was to be cleansed. It was to remove the waste within her body, just like one would take their car to a mechanic for an oil change. She quickly learned that the colonics help with so many other problems as well. When the contaminated waste is removed, it makes it easier for the body to heal."

Once I began treatment, I noticed inflammation was reduced and there was less swelling in my hands and feet. I literally felt less puffy. But most importantly, I felt good. I felt clean. I felt healthy.

"A colonic provides many benefits. It helps with PMS, promotes increased energy, the release of many different toxicants, helps your muscles relax, increases blood flow, even eventual weight loss. Your skin will be clearer; you may even notice your eyes are whiter."

After having a recent colonic, I noticed the usual dark circles under my eyes I wake up with, were gone. This girl was looking good!

"And then there are the positive side effects: It can reduce depression; help alleviate lower back and muscle pain. A person may come for one thing, such as Cheyenne who came in for a cleanse and left with many more benefits. One of which is prevention. When toxins aren't present, it can prevent cancer and other diseases from happening in the first place."

That is so true. I asked Karin to explain exactly how colon hydrotherapy works.

"We use clean, filtered, warm water. Then a small, sterilized, disposable tube is gently placed into your rectum and the water is used to loosen and remove the waste within the colon. The first treatment will mainly work on what's on the surface. I always recommend to have from 3-6 treatments to effectively clean the colon. The second, third and subsequent treatments will go much deeper and remove far more built-up waste. Depending on the age of the person, there can literally be human waste that's twenty, twenty-five, even thirty years old."

Oh yes, I saw it for myself. At first it was a dirty yellow color. That was the toxins. Then a dark muddy brown color. That was old waste. Really old nasty mud!

"When the waste is released, it flows through a clear tube that both you and I can view. My training teaches me how to quickly analyze it. I'll tell you the good, the bad and the ugly. If you've had sugar, I'm going to know. If you've been smoking, I'll be able to tell. Whatever you've put into your body will have to eventually come out. You can't hide anything from me." (She laughed as she said this!)

When I first met with Karin, I was in a lot of pain. My skin was puffy and swollen, and walking was very difficult.

"Shortly after Cheyenne started receiving regular treatments I noticed a change. She'd lost weight, she had an easier time walking and she seemed happier overall. It was great to see. Getting rid of the toxins helped reduce inflammation which helped relieve the symptoms of RA. I also consulted her on better nutrition and getting exercise; which she couldn't do before getting treatments, as it was too painful. Once she was back on her feet it made a big difference and she had a lot more energy. And with less indulgence at the lunch and dinner table, there were less toxins for me to clean out!"

I still need my Beverly Hills fine dining once in a while!

"Everything in moderation!"

But of course.

"Unfortunately, so many people wait until they're sick or diagnosed with a life-threatening illness before they see me and hope I can work a miracle. I'll always do my best to help them, but think about the person who was given six months to live because of colon cancer; it's not that they just got the cancer, they've probably had it inside them for twenty years and now it's become deadly. If only they'd had colonics and taken care of themselves twenty years ago.

I truly believe a lot of diseases could be prevented, or in my case, lessened with regular colonics. Disease starts in the gut and if the gut is clean, we're healthy. Again, it sounds simple, but it makes perfect sense. I can say for a fact that I'm a healthier, happier and more energetic person because of it.

To this day I get a colonic at least once a month.

I might still have RA, but it doesn't have me and never will!

*[1]**Karin Nahmani** holds a Bachelors in Science and credentials as a Naturopathic Doctor from Medi College in Israel. She has worked as a Certified Colon Hydrotherapist since 2001 and has owned and operated Pure Center since 2006. She is a Certified Massage Therapist and Instructor as well as a Certified Doula. http://www.purecenter.com*

If I could go back in time and
give my younger self advice…

Be Disciplined. Listen to your Body.

Stay Focused.

NINE

A Blessing In Disguise

I T'S AS IF I HAD A LIFETIME'S WORTH OF EXPERIENCES IN FOUR SHORT YEARS, starting with 2015, which was by far the darkest year of my life. I lost my best friend and the man I was in love with. I'd closed my management company and wasn't really working or doing much of anything. And then the mysterious illness that later was diagnosed as rheumatoid arthritis.

To say I was depressed wouldn't be true. I wasn't. I was lost. A lost woman trying to find herself. I didn't know what to do. I didn't know what I wanted. But I knew I had to be successful. I wanted to be the "Cheyenne Martin" I envisioned in my head, but I wasn't there yet. Not even close. I was going to have to travel great depths to find myself.

And then it happened.

I watched the documentary *The Kid Stays In The Picture* about Robert Evans. He was responsible for saving Paramount Pictures back in the '80s. It was such a compelling biopic to see this nobody, a self-proclaimed bad actor, start at the bottom and make his way to the top by hustling, aligning himself with the right individuals and having the wits to use his mouth to ask for the impossible. It was so inspiring. And that's when I knew what I wanted to do.

I was going to be a film producer.

But that doesn't just happen overnight. It takes hard work, dedication, resilience and a lot of closed doors that you have to pry open. Like Mr. Evans, I had to work my way up. I also had an illness trying to bring me down, but I wasn't going to let it.

I knew one of two things were going to happen. I was either not going to make it through to the end of the year, or God was going to push me and make straight paths for my feet. God was going to prevail. And he did.

The beginning of 2016 was a journey. I knew what was going on with me and began treatment. Things were looking up. I had a long way to go, but I was headed in the right direction. I just opened my company Emerald City Entertainment and despite being sick, I kept going; I kept working. It was very tough, but there was work to be done and I had to level up. Nothing was going to stop me, especially not RA.

When 2017 rolled around, I had some setbacks. Side effects from my RA medications threw me for a loop, big time. It was the scariest time in my life. I really thought I was losing my mind.

Before Marqese passed, I was in a dark place and he knew it. I had no focus. And if he was alive today, I know he'd be proud of me. He'd be proud of the strong business woman I've become. I would tell him about my goals of being an executive producer and a philanthropist; I have accomplished both. He would be so impressed with the woman that I've become. It still hurts that he is not here; I miss him terribly to this day.

Throughout this entire experience I learned something about myself. I learned that I can do anything I put my mind to. I've learned to educate myself on reaching goals that I want to accomplish.

Determination is one of my strongest attributes. I enjoy challenging myself to see what I can truly accomplish.

Today I feel strong. Today I am becoming the Cheyenne Martin I always wanted to be. I often say I have the strength of one hundred women. And I truly believe that.

IF I COULD TELL MY 2015 SELF ANYTHING, it would be to listen to my body. My body was telling me something was wrong, but it took me nearly a year to finally figure out what it was. Not for lack of trying, but not necessarily trying hard enough. If I could give my teenaged self advice it would be discipline. Keep your focus. I've struggled with that quite often, but with my RA diagnosis and treatment, if it taught me anything, it was to focus on your goals, whatever they may be. Don't act as though you have it all figured out. You don't. I have experienced numerous highs and lows, ups and downs. But one thing I have learned; I could not quit.

I've achieved many things and continue to pursue my goals. And there are a few regrets as well. Not so much things I have done, but things I haven't.

One regret that's always stayed with me was giving up on acting. That goes back to the early '90s. I was fortunate enough to be cast in a supporting role for Brett Ratner's first feature film as a director, *Money Talks*. That was a great experience. And I did some other work on different television shows called an Under Five (which meant you had five lines of dialogue or less). They were small roles, but it was still work and if I'd kept at it, I know I'd have gotten somewhere.

But I needed a break from LA and temporarily moved back to my hometown, Pittsburgh, and enrolled in The Pittsburgh Playhouse. And before I knew it, time had gotten away from me. And that's okay, God had other plans.

MOST OF US HAVE SAID AT ONE TIME OR ANOTHER that something is "a blessing in disguise." That couldn't be more true when it came to my RA. It was a kick in the behind and put some fire under my feet to straighten up my life. I was eating so poorly and not taking care of myself like I should. This was a much-needed wakeup call for me in so many ways. I certainly don't wish RA on anyone, but without it, I might've not even been around any longer and I certainly wouldn't be healthy and prosperous like I am today.

I've always said how strong I was. Even during the dark times, I told myself and others, "I'm strong, I'm strong!" The true test of one's strength is an experience like mine. If I could make it through this, I'm ready to take on the world!

With God's help, I rediscovered myself on this new journey. I had to lean on him for guidance and support and he was there for me. And I made it through.

That doesn't mean I can sit back and relax.

I have to continue to take care of myself. Our body is our home for our entire lives: this is where we live. We have to show it love. We have to give it healthy fuel. We respect it and it will respect us. But if you continue to abuse your body, eventually it will return the favor with pain and suffering.

So many people I know are of the "It won't happen to me" mindset. They are in for a rude awakening. Maybe not right away, but it will happen. And that's NOT going to happen to me. I learned my lesson and treat my body like a Goddess' temple.

A little indulgence now and again is fine, but it can't be an everyday thing. You have a special occasion coming up, treat yourself to something fun, something "bad." But then get back on track to your healthy lifestyle. I slip up now and then, but very rarely and I definitely get right back on track. No one wants to live in pain. No one wants to rely on others to get around. I know I don't and that's why I'm so adamant about taking care of myself.

Our gut is our second brain. You take care of it and it will not only show on the inside, it'll show on the outside. You'll feel good, and you'll look good. Our society is so focused on treating problems with medications, that often have side effects that make us feel worse than we did in the first place. I can certainly speak from experience when it comes to that. But if we're smart and we give our bodies what they need, we won't get sick in the first place. It's really that simple.

First thing each morning I pour myself a tall glass of water and add my Lypo-Spheric vitamin C. I take four collagen[1] supplements, a cup of liquid probiotics[2], a teaspoon of black seed oil[3], one garlic[4] supplement, one oregano[5] supplement and one ginger[6] supplement. A typical breakfast would be a hard-boiled egg, a piece and a half of turkey bacon, a slice of raisin bread and that starts my day. At lunch I add a turmeric supplement and my digestive enzymes[7].

Sometimes my schedule doesn't allow it, but I prefer to try and eat five smaller meals per day as opposed to the three most of us live by. It keeps your metabolism stimulated, helps with consistent energy throughout the day and maintaining a healthy weight.

And fresh is best!

WHENEVER POSSIBLE I ALWAYS GET FRESH, UNPROCESSED FOODS. Certainly not everyone can afford that, but you'd be surprised that fresh ingredients don't have to be expensive if you're smart about it. Canned foods have so many preservatives and additives that just aren't good for us. If you have to get something processed or packaged, look at the ingredients. Less is more. Look at how much sodium there is; how much sugar. Sugar is the devil!

Many of today's foods are full of artificial hormones and pesticides, which it makes it difficult, if not nearly impossible, for our bodies to break down the toxins and properly digest the food. A significant amount of sickness and diseases begin in the gut, with auto-immune diseases at an all-time high. And just because you might be young, doesn't mean you can't be affected. Auto-immune diseases don't discriminate when it comes to age.

Educate yourself as to what's good for you and what's not. Fast food and microwave dinners might seem to be cheaper, easier, faster, more convenient, but is eventually being laid up in the hospital in pain because you didn't take care of yourself worth the "convenience?" And fast food especially, is not cheap compared to what you can make at home for the same amount of cash. Try this experiment: Eat a fast food hamburger, fries and a soda and be truly honest with yourself about how you feel about an hour after. Then on another day make a healthy (but still tasty) meal at home and compare how you feel. I guarantee you'll feel significantly better. Guaranteed! And you'll probably save a few bucks in the process.

Most people think of themselves as invincible. We are not. And the sooner we realize that and take care of ourselves, the better lives we'll lead. I can't emphasize that enough. Dr. Kreitenberg has told me time and time again about patients with RA just like me who, won't change their lifestyle, won't change their bad habits and they wonder why the RA gets worse and they feel like you-know-what!

MOVING FORWARD, I plan to add a division to my charity, The Cheyenne Martin Foundation, that brings awareness to autoimmune diseases, with an emphasis on RA. I'll talk about my experiences and hope to help others, whether they've been recently diagnosed or have been living with it for a while. Although I've been through a lot in my life, I'm also fortunate to live comfortably and it's so important to me to give back.

When it comes to business, it's also very important for me to align myself with winners. Success breeds success. And first impressions are so critical. Dress to impress. No excuses.

I was once told, "If you surround yourself with nine successful people, you're bound to be the tenth." I truly believe this. My acting coach at the Pittsburgh Playhouse said, "If you believe it, your audience will believe it." I apply that philosophy to my business and everyday life.

If you look successful, you will be successful. Believe in yourself and others will believe in you.

IF I WERE TO ADVISE SOMEONE JUST STARTING OUT in the entertainment business or any business for that matter, it would be to find a mentor. Find someone who's experienced success and learn from them. Perhaps take a job as an assistant. Be diligent, work hard and impress those above you. Be that person they know is reliable, trustworthy and has a good work ethic. Someone who is self-motivated. But remember this: If you show up on time, you're late. If you start work at 9am, that means you show up at 8:45am, ready to work. No excuses. Be willing to work late, on your day off; whatever it takes. Don't just do the minimum, do the most you can and then a little bit more.

And most importantly, LISTEN! Confidence is beautiful, but inexperienced arrogance is ugly. Embrace those in positions of success who you strive to be and learn from them. Surround yourself with winners and individuals who inspire you to flourish. And whatever you do, stay away from drama. Only positive energy is allowed in your circle.

I've been blessed to have worked for some amazing people, including Barry Gordy from Motown Records. Such an amazing man. One thing that I took from my experience with him was his insistence on paper trails. He would say: "If it's not in writing, it didn't happen. Protect yourself." I couldn't agree more, especially when it comes to the entertainment business.

I've had some strong women in my life who I consider mentors. I worked with talent agent Sharon Kemp in Beverly Hills. I learned so much about representing actors, submitting them for casting breakdowns and how to close deals once they were hired. I really enjoyed this process and took it very seriously. She said, "You took to the breakdowns like Picasso took to a painting." Stephany Hurkos taught me so much about the ins-and-outs of becoming a talent manager and the entertainment business itself. She is also great at closing deals and getting top dollar for her clients. She showed me how to put together a killer package for producers and casting directors. Sheila Legette, who went from talent agent to manager, showed me how to pitch (how to present an actor you represent to a production company or casting director for consideration of a particular acting role).

I cherish my experiences with each and every one of these kind, wonderful people and the invaluable knowledge I gained from them. No school could teach me what I learned first-hand from these winners.

And when it comes to winning, there are two very important things to me: business success and personal success.

BUSINESS SUCCESS IS WHEN A FILM I'VE PRODUCED IS NOMINATED FOR AN OSCAR and it wins! To be recognized by your peers in the entertainment business is nothing short of amazing. It shows that hard work, sacrifice and turning your dreams into reality is worth every bit of blood, sweat and tears. It may take a while for this to happen, but it WILL happen and I'm ready to roll up my sleeves and get to work.

Personal success comes with me helping others. If I can help even ten people per year better their lives, whether it be battling RA; getting off the streets and starting a new, prosperous life; or just lending a hand to those in need, then I'm a success. And I look forward to sharing this success with my life partner, with my eventual husband, my king, if you will, who will be by my side and we will rule together.

I always say, "I am chasing my hero." And that hero… is me. That may sound vain, but my hero is the me that I strive be. I'm not there yet, but each day I get a little bit closer to becoming the Cheyenne Martin who's ready to take on the world.

I have so much happy & healthy life left to live, and I plan to live it to the fullest!

[1]**Collagen** *is the most abundant protein in your body. It is the major component of connective tissues that make up several body parts, including tendons, ligaments, skin and muscles. Collagen has many important functions, including providing your skin with structure and strengthening your bone. In recent years, collagen supplements have become popular. Most are hydrolyzed, which means the collagen has been broken down, making it easier for you to absorb. (Source: Heathline)*
While research is mixed, a few studies have shown collagen supplements to help with arthritis pain and sports-related joint pain. (Source: WedMD)

[2]**Probiotics** *are live microorganisms that can be consumed through fermented foods or supplements. More and more studies show that the balance or imbalance of bacteria in your digestive system is linked to overall health and disease. Probiotics promote a healthy balance of gut bacteria and have been linked to a wide range of health benefits. These include benefits for weight loss, digestive health, immune function and more. (Source: Healthline)*

[3]**Black Seed Oil.** *Historically, black seed has been used for headache, toothache, nasal congestion, asthma, arthritis, and intestinal worms. It has also been used for "pink eye" (conjunctivitis), pockets of infection (abscesses), and parasites.*

Today, black seed is most commonly used for asthma, diabetes, hypertension, and many other conditions. (Source: WebMD)

Benefits of [4]Garlic
Cholesterol & Blood Pressure Control: A review of garlic research, published in the Journal of Nutrition, analyzed studies that followed a total of more than 3,000 people. It found that garlic supplements reduced total and LDL cholesterol by up to 10 percent if taken for at least two months. Systolic blood pressure (the top number) was reduced by an average of 5.1 mm Hg, and diastolic by 2.5 mm Hg. The review also found that garlic enhanced the immune system.

Aged Garlic Extract is an Inflammation Buster: Another review, published in the Journal of Nutrition, found that other markers of atherosclerosis, such as chronic inflammation and calcification of arteries, were also reduced. Although studies showed that different types of garlic supplements were effective, researchers noted: "The most consistent benefits were shown in studies that used aged garlic extract (AGE)."

[5]**Oregano** *is used for respiratory tract disorders such as coughs, asthma, croup, and bronchitis. It is also used for gastrointestinal (GI) disorders such as heartburn and bloating. Other uses include treating menstrual cramps, rheumatoid arthritis, urinary tract disorders including urinary tract infections (UTIs), headaches, and heart conditions. (Source: WebMD)*

[6]**Ginger** *is commonly used for various types of "stomach problems," including motion sickness, morning sickness, colic, upset stomach, gas, diarrhea, irritable bowel syndrome (IBS), nausea, nausea caused by cancer treatment, nausea caused by HIV/AIDS treatment, nausea and vomiting after surgery, as well as loss of appetite.*

Other uses include pain relief from rheumatoid arthritis (RA), osteoarthritis, menstrual pain, and other conditions. However, there is not strong evidence to support the use of ginger for these conditions. (Source: WebMD)

[7]**Digestive Enzymes** *are secreted by the pancreas and aid the body in breaking down fats, proteins, and carbohydrates. When normal functioning of the pancreas is disrupted (due to illness or injury) resulting in insufficient enzyme production, the body may be unable to properly absorb these nutrients. Digestive enzyme supplements are thought to protect against this malabsorption.*

In addition, proteolytic enzymes are said to lower cholesterol. Although digestive enzymes are normally taken with meals for digestive purposes, when taken in between meals on an empty stomach, they are said to stimulate the immune system, manage arthritis, reduce inflammation, improve liver health, and fight cancer. (Source: Very Well Health)

TEN

The Reality

ONTRARY TO WHAT MANY PEOPLE THINK, rheumatoid arthritis (RA) is not traditional arthritis. It's not an old person's disease; I'm certainly not old! RA can come at any time in your life, even as a teenager.

I'll let the experts at the Arthritis Foundation tell you a little more about it:

What is RA?

Rheumatoid arthritis is an autoimmune disease in which the body's immune system—which normally protects its health by attacking foreign substances like bacteria and viruses—mistakenly attacks the joints. This creates inflammation that causes the tissue that lines the inside of joints (the synovium) to thicken, resulting in swelling and pain in and around the joints. The synovium makes a fluid that lubricates joints and helps them move smoothly.

If inflammation goes unchecked, it can damage cartilage, the elastic tissue that covers the ends of bones in a joint, as well as the bones themselves. Over time, there is loss of cartilage, and the joint spacing between bones can become smaller. Joints can become loose, unstable, painful and lose their mobility. Joint deformity also can occur. Joint damage cannot be reversed, and because it can occur early, doctors recommend early diagnosis and aggressive treatment to control RA.

Rheumatoid arthritis most commonly affects the joints of the hands, feet, wrists, elbows, knees and ankles.

The joint effect is usually symmetrical. That means if one knee or hand is affected, usually the other one is, too. Because RA also can affect body systems, such as the cardiovascular or respiratory systems, it is called a systemic disease. Systemic means "entire body."

Who's Affected by Rheumatoid Arthritis?

About 1.5 million people in the United States have RA. Nearly three times as many women have the disease as men. In women, RA most commonly begins between ages 30 and 60. In men, it often occurs later in life. Having a family member with RA increases the odds of having RA; however, the majority of people with RA have no family history of the disease.

IF, AFTER READING THIS BOOK, YOU THINK YOU MIGHT HAVE RA, please check with your doctor and see what he or she has to say. This disease can be tricky to diagnose, so if you still think something's wrong after that visit, it might be worth it to get a second opinion.

It's your body and your life — you deserve the very best.

AFTERWORD

By Craig Jace CTN, DOM, LAc, PA

TRADITIONAL ALLOPATHIC MEDICINE for autoimmune diseases have changed very little since I started my holistic wellness center in 1998. When Cheyenne asked me to write the afterword to this book, I was delighted to acknowledge and agreed with the alternative path she eventually undertook to quell the signs and symptoms of a devastating disease.

As you have read in her previous chapters, Cheyenne illustrated the many facets of chronic illness where mental and physical functions intertwine, in which the end result can be healing or succumbing to disease. Every individual plays a vital role in how the mind/body connection can greatly affect the outcome of our health. In Cheyenne's case, she battled the autoimmune disease called Rheumatoid Arthritis. Autoimmune disease is becoming more prevalent, in fact, it is over three times more common than just decades ago. This finding is not due to an increased recognition or changes in diagnostic criteria, but actual new cases of autoimmune disease are appearing.

Researchers are finding that increased exposure to environmental toxins, infections, stress and the common American diet are contributing to the increased autoimmunity so prevalent in the medical community today. Cheyenne has given us a unique perspective on what has been successful for her. Even though what has worked for Cheyenne's unique constitution may not solve another person's chronic illness, this book does give the reader hope and insight to begin their own path to wellness.

Hopefully, books like this will open one's eyes to improving their health while combating disease. Holistic, alternative and conventional medicine are not mutually exclusive. Conventional medicine is often necessary and lifesaving until more natural therapies can be instituted to build the body's natural defense mechanisms.

This was one patient's story I hope you enjoyed!

About The Author

CHEYENNE MARTIN GREW UP IN PITTSBURGH, PA blessed with a mother who encouraged her to express herself. At the age of 6, she first experienced the thrill of hearing the crowd's applause while modeling at fashion shows alongside her mother. Shortly after, she officially began modeling, started acting in plays like *Little Orphan Annie* and competed in talent shows, often taking first place.

Ms. Martin attended Contra Costa College, but had her sights set on becoming an actress. Always one to pursue her dreams, with unstoppable determination, she headed straight out of Pittsburgh to Los Angeles.

Shortly after arriving in Los Angeles, she began working for the legendary Berry Gordy of Motown Records as well as Jobete Publishing. She was instrumental in organizing the "Motown 30" celebration with several of the stars. Her other early positions were with Fox News, and soon after, alongside Rapper Heavy D as his personal assistant.

Although she was having success and a good time, she realized that she needed to focus on what she moved to Los Angeles to do, which was acting. She started studying with acting coach Al Guarino, and soon she was being cast in films. Although she enjoyed acting, the experience began to entice her into a different direction. She had an urge go behind the scenes and camera. This revelation propelled her further in life and into a very exciting, new dimension in her entertainment career.

Cheyenne was hired by the "LA Confidential" record label, where she learned the recording industry inside and out. Soon she was working for various record labels and agents. Then as an agent's assistant for Sharon Kemp of the Sharon Kemp Talent Agency and with talent manager Stephany Hurkos. With this invaluable experience under her belt, Ms. Martin was ready to take the next step and go out on her own as a talent manager.

SHE ESTABLISHED HER FIRST COMPANY IN 2007, Cheyenne Martin Management. Having been an actress herself, she understood the highs and lows of the acting profession and her agency was successful. Known for her innovative and pioneering spirit; she kicks up her high heels, takes her celebrity connections and friendships, and mixes them with her east coast hustle and drive to forge successes for all her clientele.

In 2014, she became Executive Producer for the film *Message from a Mistress*, a tale of three wives who are harboring secrets and then have their worlds rocked when they learn that one of their husbands is having an affair with their widowed best friend. The success of this film lead to a decision by Cheyenne to launch yet another phase of her career and in 2016, she established her film company, Emerald City Entertainment.

In addition to her successful entertainment career, Cheyenne Martin is also a philanthropist and in 2015 founded The Cheyenne Martin Foundation. This non-profit organization mentors and empowers women in the underserved and underrepresented communities throughout the Los Angeles and Pittsburgh areas.

Presently Ms. Martin has numerous projects in the works with a very bright future ahead of her.

I would like to gratefully acknowledge:

Sean Michael Beyer for being by my side through this entire writing process,

keeping me focused and on schedule; I couldn't have done it without you.

Dr. Adam Kreitenberg for helping me understand and effectively treat RA.

Dr. Craig Jace for starting me on the path of holistic health and wellness.

Karin Nahmani for assisting me on this journey and teaching me about my body

and how important it is to rid oneself of toxins.

Nancy Mura for your help during physical therapy and for introducing me to Dr. Jace.

I'd also like to thank the following wonderful people:

To my son Dre Bowie and my granddaughter Tamia, I love you guys; Tiffany Bowie, I love being your big sister; Donnie Bowie, you're my big little brother. Taylor Bowie, you're my heartbeat; Melva Fitzgerald, I've admired you my whole life; Marva Hughes, you're the most solid and honest woman I've known in my lifetime; Patti Cook, I've admired your beauty and wit since I was a child; Kimberley Hemmingway, we're more than cousins, we're like sisters who spend hours on the phone laughing. You're one of my best cousins; I love you and the kids. Sweetie Sherrie, your conversations and strength inspire me, and I love you and Bianca Sky; Chanel Jones Harris, I've loved you since you were a baby and I'm proud of the women you have grown to be. I love the Harris family; Ky Ziegler, you have been with me on this journey and you've been solid. Thanks for being my non-biological sister; Nikki Cain, you know where all my bones are buried. We've been through so much together. You're such a strong women who always prevails. You inspire me; Chasity Clark, your heart is pure. I admire your business savvy and strength. Thanks for always being there for me; Jason Lee, the one and only. You taught me how to bounce, not fall. You inspire me for your resilience, tenacity and determination; Sanya Bowie, my cousin who I admire for her strength; Andre Bowie, you've always been like a second brother to me; Donnika Bowie, my niece who is my twin, I've loved you since I laid eyes on you; my nephew Mook Pie, continue to be you, I applaud your strength; Dale Settles, make straight paths for

your feet, I believe in you; Nitra Sledge, we've been through so many fun times

together; Dennis Fitzgerald, you always teased me and I love you for that; Tanya

Fitzgerald, we grew up like sisters and fought like brothers, but I love you to death;

Kieren Boyce, thanks for coming to me with a torch when I was in the dark a

few times; Amanda Hardy, the Godmother to my son, I've known more than half

my life. You always had my back in a crunch; Kathy Ware, a great women who I

admire; Nita Perry, we've been friends since thirteen years old. You always have

my best

interests at heart. We always have a great time when hanging out. To my uncles

Dr. Stan L. Bowie, Jack Bowie, Micheal Bowie and Wayne Handy, I love you all

dearly;

Annie Boyd, my aunt who has always been there to cheer me on; Gemini

Huffman, my cousin, we just met a year ago and we clicked like perfect pieces of a

puzzle; Roberta,

I enjoy our talks about being better women; Kelly Littlejohn, thanks for being there

for me, my mom and sister; Elicia Surles, thanks for always coming through; and

last, but not least, my mentors: Shelia Legette, Sharon Kemp and Stephany Hurkos.

I'm glad God brought each and every one of you into my life.

I love you all.

There are over 100 known
autoimmune diseases
and I have one of them.

My name is Cheyenne Martin
and I have Rheumatoid Arthritis.

But it doesn't have me.

Printed in the United States
By Bookmasters